Copyright © 2024 Laura S. Martin

All rights reserved

The characters and events portrayed in this book are fictitious. Any similarity to real persons, living or dead, is coincidental and not intended by the author.

No part of this book may be reproduced, or stored in a retrieval system, or transmitted in any form or by any means, electronic, mechanical, photocopying, recording, or otherwise, without express written permission of the publisher.

ISBN-13: 9798304037518

Cover design by: Art Painter
Library of Congress Control Number: 2018675309
Printed in the United States of America

*To my dear friend Andrea who dreamed of
calling out the service industry with me for
MANY years. To all of the amazing co-workers I
have served with and companies I have learned
from, the good and the bad and to the future
of the service industry. I believe in you!*

# CONTENTS

Copyright
Dedication
Introduction   1
Chapter 1   4
Chapter 2   9
Chapter 3   15
Chapter 4   21
Chapter 5   27
Chapter 6   33
Chapter 7   41
Chapter 8   50
Chapter 9   59
Chapter 10   72
Chapter 11   79

# INTRODUCTION

Why is customer service still one of the most talked-about topics in business books, workplace manuals, and seminars? Because, despite all the discussion, training, and best intentions, we just can't seem to get it right.

As toddlers, we learned the basics of customer service when the lady at the grocery store handed us a lollipop or a sticker as Mom checked out. We didn't know much, but we knew one thing—she made us happy. We wanted to go back. We wanted Mom to choose *her lane.*

Fast-forward to today. What's the bar now? Well, if we survive a transaction unscathed—no yelling, no passive-aggressive glares, and no physical altercations—it's practically a five-star experience. When did we decide this was acceptable?

The truth is, most of us would like to think we don't spend money foolishly, but let's face it: if we really want that shiny new cell phone, we'll tolerate the surly, disengaged salesperson. We'll grit our teeth, take the abuse, and hand over our hard-earned cash because, apparently, that's the deal we've accepted in our current society.

Especially through my travels, I've seen customer service horrors that could make the most patient among us snap. And while there are many industries that deserve a stern talking-to, one in particular consistently gets my blood boiling: the airline industry.

Oh, the airlines. And one airline in particular. Let's call it F------ Airlines. You know the one. Somehow, this carrier has set the standard for service so bad, it's almost an art form. Which leads me to wonder: what must their meetings be like?

This book explores the fictional, purely imaginary (of course!) meetings that must have taken place at a business similar to F------ Airlines to concoct their customer "service" policies. These aren't real meetings, but let's be honest: they might as well be. If you've ever waited on hold for hours, endured endless delays with zero communication, or been charged extra for daring to breathe on a flight, you'll recognize the spirit of these meetings immediately.

But this isn't just about airlines. This is about all businesses that seem to have collectively decided customer service is optional. I hope as you read, you will not be stuck in the airline scenario. Think about how the principles affect your business, your employment and your experience as a customer. In these pages, we'll look at how corner-cutting policies get cooked up, what they mean for customers and employees alike, and—most importantly—what could be done differently.

This book is purposely short. We need to be reminded of why customer service is important, get to the point and then get back to serving people. I believe the concise format of this book will be valuable to you without all the extra fluff.

Through sarcasm, storytelling, and a touch of righteous indignation, I hope to spark a conversation about the service we've come to accept and the service we deserve to give AND receive. You may not be in the airlines industry but whether you're a business owner, a manager, or simply a weary traveler, my hope is that this book inspires you to demand better—and maybe even *do* better.

Now, shall we crash (ahem, attend) their first meeting?

# CHAPTER 1
## Honesty and Transparency

The year is 2002. The airline industry is in chaos, scrambling to recover from the catastrophic impact of 9/11 a few short months earlier. Profits are plummeting, and executives are panicking. Some airlines, like Southwest, were fortunate enough to receive heartfelt letters and even checks from loyal customers eager to help keep them stay afloat.

But at F------ Airlines, desperation had taken a different form. They weren't banking on loyalty or goodwill. No, they were holding a brainstorming meeting, the kind where "big ideas" and questionable morals collided.

"We are at a pivotal moment," began the accountant-slash-CFO wannabe, a man whose pocket protector gleamed with ambition.

"We need ideas. Big ones. Ideas that not only keep us in business but grow the business. The secret," he added with a conspiratorial smirk, "is that our customers can't know we're growing. They need to believe we're barely surviving, hanging on by a thread, all for their benefit. We must convince them we're on *their side*."

The room buzzed with nervous excitement.

"What if," the accountant said, pausing for dramatic effect, "we charged the lowest possible fare?"

A hush fell over the room, confusion clouding every face. Was this man advocating for charity work?

"Here's the trick," he continued, his eyes gleaming with glee. "We sell tickets dirt cheap, so when passengers compare prices, we're always the cheapest. *Always.* But—" he raised a finger, "—if they want anything beyond the ticket that gets them through security, we charge them. For everything. Want to bring a suitcase? Fee. Want to pick your seat? Fee, fee, fee. It'll be a masterpiece!"

The room erupted in cheers. Executives high-fived, already envisioning their fat bonuses.

"And don't forget," the accountant shouted over the applause, "I believe we can make the seats smaller to fit in more seats to sell. People won't complain—they'll blame themselves for being too big!"

A few attendees laughed uncomfortably.

The meeting adjourned, the executives smug and satisfied, ready to revolutionize the industry... one tiny, overpriced step at a time.

## What Happens When You Nickel-and-Dime Your Customers?

In that hypothetical meeting, do you think anyone paused to ask, "Is this what our customers deserve?" Probably not. At F------ Airlines, the "nickel-and-dime" strategy became their signature move. Sure, the $29 ticket from Denver to Las Vegas sounds like a steal—until you realize it only buys you a hard seat in the back of the plane, where not even a smile is included. Want to bring more than a toothbrush and clean underwear? That'll cost extra.

This isn't just frustrating; it's borderline deceitful. Customers are lured in with an enticingly low fare, only to discover the real cost as the fees pile up. The result? Stress and resentment before they've even reached the gate.

So, what's the alternative? How do businesses avoid this trap while still managing costs?

## Trust vs. Profit

F------ Airlines may have succeeded in drawing in customers with rock-bottom fares, but at what cost? The barrage of extra fees erodes trust, leaving customers feeling tricked. And while that $29 fare might win the initial sale, it's unlikely to generate repeat business—or glowing reviews on social media that take years to remedy.

In contrast, businesses that prioritize transparency

and fairness earn long-term loyalty. It is not about being perfect; it's about creating a consistent, positive experience. Customers will forgive mistakes if they believe you are genuinely trying to do right by them.

**Lessons for Leaders**

If you are a leader, ask yourself: Are you setting a standard of mediocrity or excellence? The choice you make ripples through your organization, influencing not just profits but the morale and trust of your customers and employees.

At the end of the day, service is not just about avoiding complaints—it's about creating advocates. Businesses that embrace this mindset will thrive, while those that treat customers as cash cows will find themselves losing ground.

---

**Takeoff or Crash Landing?**

So, back to F------ Airlines. Their low-cost strategy may fill seats, but the mistrust it generates leaves customers fuming before the plane even leaves the ground. And the connection between profits and service? Completely mangled.
The moral of the story? Excellence in service is not a luxury; it's a necessity. Customers do not just want a good deal—they want to feel valued, respected, and understood.

**Reviews of the F------ airline are overwhelming complaints that after paying fees for EVERYTHING, they paid more than what they would have had they chose another carrier with higher up-front charges.**

# CHAPTER 2
## Stay on Mission

"The profits are off the charts now that we charge the customer for every service and tangible item they get from us," the newly promoted CFO announced as he opened the meeting.

His face radiated with the kind of smug satisfaction only achievable by someone who has never been stranded in an airport without a snack.

Cheers and applause erupted in the room.

"But what can we do to *save and grow* the money that's rolling in?" he continued, adjusting his tie as though he were preparing for a televised victory speech.

"Let's go around the room and hear your ideas. Claire, let's begin with you."

Claire from Marketing adjusted her glasses and offered with pride, "We could ask our current customers to share our monthly specials with their email contacts. For every ten people they spam—I mean, reach out to—they'll receive a dollar off their next flight with us!"

The CFO nodded. "Excellent! Leveraging free labor from our own customers and now we have a barrage of potential customer email addresses. Very clever, Claire. Mark, you're up next."

Mark from Operations, clearly angling for a promotion, leaned forward. "At my former company, we saved a lot of money by outsourcing customer service overseas. We encouraged customers to contact our convenient 1-800 number for any and all issues. It didn't matter if the agents got it wrong, because we gave them detailed scripts and templates to follow that they were not permitted to stray from. It was cost-effective *and* avoided too much pesky human connection!"

Kelly chimed in, "we could even charge a fee if you want to talk with an agent."

The CFO's face lit up. "That's it, Mark! Let's do it! Kelly, I love that idea! Service Managers, start drafting layoff plans for the American team. This meeting is adjourned!"

The room burst into applause again, echoing with the kind of enthusiasm usually reserved for an open bar at a company holiday party.

## We Are Happy to Take Care of You—Please Hold

I admit it: I like big-box stores. I walk in, grab what I need, and no store associates hover over me. It is efficient, and I know where everything is. If I do need help, it's usually because something heavy is on a shelf too high for my 5-foot-2 stature to reach.

But there are some situations where service matters —where service *is* the product.

Most people are self-sufficient. We don't want to ask for help unless absolutely necessary. But when we do, we want the service to meet our personal "white glove" standards.

Everyone has a different standard for their particular white glove service. My "white glove" for the bank involves me calling, hearing a friendly human say, "Hello, Laura," and having my issue resolved without the dreaded "let me transfer you to the right department."

Contrast that with my "white glove" experience at some call centers. You know the drill: You call because you have no other choice. You have tried to figure it out on your own, you have gone online but you can't get your issue resolved.

Now you've cleared your schedule, mentally prepared yourself, donned your battle armor, and made the call. You have entered your account number, the last 4 digits of your social security number, date of birth, blood type and anything else they dream of asking *at least* three times on your keypad.

The cheerful voice assuring you, "Your call is very important to us," starts to feel like a personal insult after the tenth minute on hold.

Finally, a person answers. You exhale, thinking your ordeal is almost over—only for them to ask for the same information you just punched into your phone three times. Blood boiling, you repeat it. Then, you share your problem, only to hear the words that make every customer's heart sink: "I'll need to transfer you to the right department."

Cue the sharp-object removal protocol from your immediate space.

Why do companies put customers through this? Cost-saving measures, of course. But here's the thing: Empowering employees to resolve issues *on the spot* doesn't just make customers happy—it builds trust.

If you operate a business that relies on a 1-800 number for customer service, consider the following:

1. **Hire employees who understand your customers' language and culture.** This includes slang, common phrases, and the tone customers expect. No one wants to feel like their concerns are being lost in

translation.

2. **Train and trust your employees to solve problems.** Empower them with the tools, authority, and confidence to offer real solutions. Give them clear objectives—whether it's minimizing refunds, avoiding negative reviews, or retaining customer loyalty—and let them act.

3. **Avoid cookie-cutter responses.** Customers can spot insincerity a mile away. Saying, "I understand your frustration, and I'm happy to assist" means nothing if it sounds robotic. Instead, teach employees to engage authentically:
   - "That sounds frustrating. Let's figure this out together."
   - "I can see why that's annoying—let me get this resolved for you."
   - "I've been there myself; here's what we can do."

Refunds and freebies aren't always the answer. What customers want most is acknowledgment, effort, resolution and a sense that their business is valued.

Take the fictional F------ Airline, for example. They see outsourcing and call scripts as cost-saving wins, but what they're really saving is pennies at the expense of dollars (and trust). The control they try to have can actually cost them money.

When customers finally get off hold, they're frustrated. When they have been transferred five times, they're livid. And when their problem remains unresolved, they're unlikely to ever use this company again—and eager to warn others not to either.

Great service is not about perfection. It's about consistency, empathy, and turning problems into opportunities to build loyalty. Companies that empower employees to act in the customer's best interest won't just avoid rants on social media—they'll create raving fans who stick around for the long haul.

Isn't that worth more than a 30-minute wait on hold?

**Reviews of the F------ airline are overwhelming complaints that when having to call the 800 number for a resolution, the agent could not be understood due to a language difference which led to a lack of communication in general. Other reviews were that the agent told the customer that "there was nothing I could do."**

# CHAPTER 3
## What is True Value?

Junior, the eager state college graduate trying to climb the corporate ladder, sat rigidly in the meeting room, sandwiched between two directors who smelled faintly of leather briefcases and self-importance. The CFO, standing at the head of the table, beamed like a proud chef unveiling a soufflé that hadn't collapsed.

"We're now officially number one!" the CFO declared. "When customers search for the lowest airfare online, we're *always* the first choice!"

The room erupted in cheers. High-fives all around.

Someone popped a bottle of sparkling water—well, they would have if it weren't a meeting at *this* airline, where beverages, even in the office, required a voucher.

"And that's not all," the CFO continued, leaning in for effect. "Once the customer purchases their dirt-cheap ticket, they log on to our site to discover our irresistible *bundles*: checked baggage, carry-ons, and seat selection—just $185 extra! Pure profit, ladies and gentlemen. Pure profit."

The room exploded with applause like the CFO had just reinvented air travel itself. Even the intern in the corner clapped enthusiastically, despite not understanding what "pure profit" actually meant.

Junior, perched awkwardly on his chair, hesitated. His palms were sweaty, but this was his chance. He raised his trembling hand, clearing his throat.

"Excuse me, sir," Junior began, his voice cracking slightly, "what happens once passengers are on the plane? They're tired, and flying dehydrates people. What if we offered them a combo deal—a drink and a snack—for just $2.99? I mean, soft drinks and peanuts aren't free for us, so why should they be for them? Logical passengers wouldn't expect freebies after paying just $29 for a ticket, right?"

The room fell silent. Junior's heart raced as the CFO stared at him with an expression so unreadable it could have been either a million-dollar Vegas winning poker face or an existential crisis.

Finally, the CFO broke into a slow, deliberate clap.

"Junior," he said, his voice brimming with approval, "see me in my office after this meeting. That's the best idea I've heard since we started charging for carry-ons!"

The room erupted once more, this time with

hoots and hollers. Junior beamed, basking in his moment of glory, while silently wondering if he'd just invented the airline's next customer relations disaster.

---

On a recent flight with F------ Airline, I mean, another airline that started with the letter "F", I watched in secondhand embarrassment as the flight attendants awkwardly shuffled down the aisle, tray in hand.

"Can I offer you a snack and a beverage for $2.99?" they repeated robotically at each row.

The passengers' reactions varied. Some rolled their eyes. Others declined curtly. A few actually reached for their wallets, though their expressions suggested they'd rather be donating a kidney.

*Really?* I thought to myself. *Is this what airline hospitality has come to?* From the 1950's to the 1970's, flying commercially was a luxury and passengers were treated with respect and dignity. Flying was a glamorous affair. Passengers dressed in their finest attire, and flight attendants, often young, healthy and stylish, exuded elegance in their designer uniforms. They provided attentive service, catering to passengers' needs. While onboard smoking was permitted, (which I am happy about this one big improvement of its ban) it was a different era, a time when air travel was a special occasion.

Nothing about this airline's approach said, "We value your business." Instead, it screamed, "How much more can we squeeze out of you before landing?"

The flight attendants, bless them, tried to soften the blow. "Or," they added sheepishly, "would you like a cup of water?"

*A cup of water?* It felt less like an offering and more like a subtle test of my dignity. I stayed silent, unwilling to risk being charged for the cup—or worse, insulted for the audacity of asking. I made a mental note to never forget my refillable water bottle again while traveling.

My parched throat and growing headache only heightened my suspicion that the lavatory might soon feature a coin-operated slot.

This airline could learn a thing or two from Bob Farrell, the visionary behind Farrell's Ice Cream Parlors, whose mantra was simple: *"Give 'em the pickle."* Farrell's philosophy wasn't about literal pickles; it was about small gestures that made customers feel valued. If someone wanted an extra pickle, you gave it to them—no charge, no drama. His logic was clear: businesses aren't just about products; they're about *people.*

After Farrell retired, corporate executives took over his business. Predictably, things went south. Why? Because they replaced Farrell's heart-first approach with spreadsheets and profit margins.

And that is precisely what's happening with F------ Airline. Somewhere along the line, the "corporate types" forgot what it's like to be a customer—especially one on a budget.

Sure, customers are lured in by low ticket prices, but the bait-and-switch tactics leave them feeling exploited and unimportant.

Here's the thing: it's not just the $2.99 for snacks that leaves customers sour. It's the principle. When every interaction feels like a transaction, customers start to feel like marks in a con game. It's the same sinking feeling you get when you realize you just overpaid for a lemon at a used car lot.

Farrell's "pickle philosophy" wasn't about generosity for generosity's sake. It was about creating value beyond the product. It's the little things—a complimentary beverage, a genuine smile, a sincere "thank you for flying with us"—that cost next to nothing but create loyal customers who *want* to return.

The truth is people understand (for the most part) that businesses need to make a profit to survive. But if profit is the sole motivation, that business won't last. Customers aren't obstacles to revenue; they're the reason for it.

Companies that truly thrive are the ones motivated by service. Profits follow naturally when businesses focus on the human connection. It's about turning rants into raves, complaints into compliments, and one-time transactions into lifelong relationships.

So, to every business—especially F------ Airline—here's the challenge: stop obsessing over the bottom line and start obsessing over your customers. Because in the end, they're the only bottom line that matters.

**Reviews on that F------airline are overwhelming complaints about the egregious fees for baggage, the change fees which can be up to triple the cost of the original ticket, and the audacity of the snack fees. Some passengers feel like employees are paid an extra bonus for charging the passenger more at the gate. If the airline doesn't go out of business, customers feel they might expect a restroom charge in the near future.**

# CHAPTER 4
## It's All About the Small Things

"Good morning, everyone!" The CFO beamed; his tone cheerful enough to make you almost forget he was about to drop another cost-cutting idea on his team.

"First off, thank you for all your hard work. Our plans are rolling out perfectly, and if this continues, I see substantial Christmas bonuses in your futures.

Today, I'd like to focus on the details. You see, once our customers are on the plane, their money is already in our bank, and there isn't much they can do about it. We don't want them to feel guilty about their decision to give us their money.

Here's the challenge: we need them to feel like we care about the little things—even if we don't actually *do* much. Let's brainstorm ways to convince them we're all about attention to detail."

The room buzzed with anticipation.

"Junior," the CFO said, zeroing in on the eager young employee. "What brilliant idea do you have for me today?"

Junior sat up straight, his tie slightly askew but his enthusiasm unwavering. "Well," he began nervously, "they say 'image is everything,' right? What if our brand radiated warmth and likability? Almost everyone loves animals. What if we decorated each of our planes with a cute animal theme?

You know, like one plane could be the Koala Plane, another could be the Dolphin Plane. We could even incorporate these themes into our FAA-mandated safety demos: 'Welcome aboard the Koala Plane! Did you know koalas sleep 20 hours a day? Sit back, relax, and embrace your inner koala.'"

The CFO squinted, clearly intrigued.

Junior pressed on. "And, here's the kicker: we turn it into a loyalty game. Passengers could try to fly on all the animal-themed planes—kind of like collecting trading cards but with boarding passes. It's a low-cost detail that makes us seem creative and fun."

The CFO nodded slowly, then broke into a wide grin. "Junior, you've done it again! Brilliant! This is exactly the kind of 'attention to detail' that will keep them coming back for more! Great work!"

The room erupted into applause. Junior blushed and

muttered a bashful "thank you."

---

## It's All About the Small Things

Years ago, comedian and podcaster Joe Rogan had a joke with a punchline that went something like this: "Putting stickers of dolphins and unicorns on it doesn't make it beautiful." Even if you haven't heard the joke (which would not be appropriate for me to repeat in this book), you get the point. You can't hide the ugly truth with cute distractions.

This is where the "details" matter. Not the superficial stickers and koala mascots, but the kind that genuinely improve someone's experience.

For me personally, those details are the small gestures that make you feel remembered and appreciated—like when a client sends you a box of cookies for Christmas or even when a barista spells your name correctly without asking. They are tiny investments that create lasting impressions.

The same applies to businesses. Imagine picking up your car from the repair shop and finding an unexpected dog treat on the seat for your pup. You didn't ask for it, but it made your day (and your pup happy too). Now contrast that with being charged an extra $3 at the checkout for some random "convenience fee."

One makes you feel special; the other makes you feel like you've been fleeced.

When it comes to airlines, these "details" can make or break the experience.

I've flown on carriers that hand out complimentary quality snacks and full cans of soda, and even though I rarely consume either, I still felt pampered. It wasn't the snack itself—it was the thought. They said, "Here's something for you, on us." And that little gesture left me feeling valued versus feeling like a burden for wanting more than 4 ounces of soda.

But let's talk about that F------ airline. They don't just withhold the small details; they actively erase them. Like seats that don't recline that ¼ inch unless you've forked over $185 for the privilege. When you're on a flight for hours, trapped in an upright position, you can't help but think, *Why do you hate me?*

Then there's the seat padding—or lack thereof. Who signed off on that design? I can only imagine the CEO as a cartoon villain, rubbing his hands together in glee: *"Let's make them pay for extra comfort! Mwahaha!"*

Despite how you feel about the green environmental movement, being charged more to offset your carbon emissions is not going to change the world. This particular airline has manipulative signage that says, "We charge for bags to encourage travelers to pack thoughtfully and in turn help us reduce our carbon footprint. In fact, changes like this helped us become 39% more fuel efficient than the other airlines- that saved them 102 million gallons of fuel" and "Seats have been carefully designed to maximize space and comfort. More importantly, they are lightweight which saves millions of gallons of fuel each year. This means you save some green by going green." And "we are proud of our tiny tray tables to be lightweight".

Perhaps not everyone can see through what they are actually saying but what I see is similar to, "we don't offer water to help prevent overloading your kidneys". Thanks, but I don't need that kind of help.

Here's the truth: attracting new customers is hard. But keeping the ones you already have? That should not be even harder. The easiest way to lose them is by neglecting the little things that make them feel valued.

In their book *Raving Fans*, Ken Blanchard and Sheldon Bowles introduce the concept of "plus one percent." The idea is simple: start by being consistent in what you offer. Then, once you've mastered consistency, improve by just one percent. You don't have to go from mediocre to Michelin-starred overnight. You just have to do a little better, every day.

Imagine if F------ airline decided to take this approach. They wouldn't have to start handing out lobster dinners at 30,000 feet. A simple snack, a smile from the flight attendants, or a modestly reclining seat might be enough to turn their passengers into loyal fans. Instead, it seems that they revert backwards one percent.

In the end, it's not about the snacks, the koalas, or even the reclined seats. It's about what those things represent: that someone, somewhere in the company, cares about the customer. And that's a detail worth flying for.

**Reviews on the F------airline are overwhelming complaints about putting profits before people, agents who put forth no effort to provide "above and beyond" service and the smallest gesture of all, refreshments on board.**

# CHAPTER 5
## Communication and Integrity

"Good morning, team!" the CFO bellowed as he strode into the room, holding a clipboard like it was the scepter of corporate authority.

"We've got a situation," he continued, eyes narrowing as though he'd just uncovered a mutiny. "It seems our customers—brace yourselves—are *complaining*. I know! The audacity!"

He slammed the clipboard on the table for dramatic effect, though nobody flinched. This was, after all, a Tuesday.

"We're offering them the *lowest fares in the industry*. And what do we get in return? Emails! Phone calls! Social media rants! These people actually expect… service! Can anyone explain why they aren't ecstatic about what we're doing here?"

Silence filled the room, thick enough to cut with the plastic knives from the breakroom.

"Well? Anyone?"

The team exchanged looks, each secretly hoping to avoid eye contact with the CFO. Finally, Junior, emboldened by a false sense of confidence (or perhaps a second latte), raised a hand.
"Maybe... maybe they're mad because we don't tell them what's going on?"

The CFO glared. "What are you implying, Junior? That honesty and communication *matter*? Preposterous!" He rolled his eyes and muttered, "This generation."

---

## *Communication and Integrity*

In my personal life, I admit I do not excel at communicating with those close to me. After a long day of problem-solving and people-managing, the last thing I want to do is deep-dive into how my loved ones felt about their sandwich at lunch or dissect the plot of the latest TV show they are watching just to have some basic conversation.

When it comes to communication, my masculine energy is king. I'm all about the facts: what happened, when, and how do we fix it?

But while my personal relationships have (mostly) survived my no-nonsense communication style, businesses don't have that luxury. Clear, honest communication isn't optional—it's essential.

A lack of communication in business does not just frustrate people; it leaves them feeling undervalued and disrespected. The number one customer complaint is almost always some variation of: *"They didn't tell me."* The missing piece of information —whether it's about a delay, a price increase, or a mistake—creates a vacuum. And nature, as we all know, abhors a vacuum. Customers will fill that silence with worst-case scenarios: *Are they hiding something? Did they forget about me? Are they manipulating me? Do they even care?*

Take airlines, for example. We all know stuff happens: weather, mechanical issues, the occasional flight attendant calling out sick. Nobody likes delays, but we tolerate them better when the airline communicates clearly, promptly, and sincerely.

Here's what effective communication looks like in practice:

- **Tell the customer what happened.** Use real words, not jargon. ("A minor maintenance issue" is better than "an operational irregularity.")

- **Explain what you're doing about it.** Offering a solution—even if it's imperfect—reassures customers that you care.

- **Apologize sincerely.** "We're sorry for the inconvenience" has been overplayed but can be accepted. A heartfelt "We know this was not how you wanted to spend your day, so we are going to remedy it as quickly as possible" is more honest and goes a long way. Add a small gesture of goodwill, like a meal voucher, and you'll turn anger into loyalty.

Contrast that with the all-too-common airline approach: saying nothing, shrugging off complaints, or worse, blaming the customer. When customers feel ignored or mistreated, they're not just done with you—they'll tell everyone they know.

---

**The Power of Proactive Service**

I am a sucker for infomercials and fell in love with a makeup company, Il Makiage. They nailed customer service. I placed an order, then promptly forgot about it (because makeup is not exactly my life's passion). A few days later, I received an email from the company apologizing for a shipping delay I hadn't even noticed. They owned the problem and gave me a generous discount and a free gift for the inconvenience.

That simple, proactive gesture turned me into a lifelong customer. I didn't even care about the delay—it wasn't on my radar—but their preemptive communication showed me they valued my business.

What's funny is that I don't even wear much makeup. Yet here I am, spending much more than what I'd normally spend because of their exceptional service. That is the power of communication and integrity: it builds trust and loyalty.

## Preparing for the Inevitable

The truth is mistakes and disruptions are inevitable in any business. What sets great companies apart is how they prepare for and respond to those moments. Here are a few questions every organization should consider:

- Do you have contingency plans for common problems?
- Are your employees empowered to resolve issues without needing a manager's approval?
- Have you trained your team to communicate clearly and empathetically with customers, even in difficult situations?

Building loyalty isn't just about avoiding mistakes—it's about how you handle them when they happen. By addressing issues head-on, communicating with integrity, and taking proactive steps to make things right, you can transform frustrated customers into your biggest advocates.

In a world where most businesses scramble to do the bare minimum, be the one that goes the extra mile. Communicate better. Apologize sincerely. And most importantly, show your customers that they matter —not just in words, but in action.

Because at the end of the day, that's what separates the companies we tolerate from the ones we rave about.

**Reviews of the F------ airline are overwhelming complaints that when flights were cancelled or delayed, they were given a piece of paper with the customer's choice of resolution, neither which were acceptable to the customer - especially since in some markets, this airline only has flights to certain destinations a few times a week. Customers were left stranded in cities where they knew no one or had to pay out of pocket for other accommodations.**

# CHAPTER 6
## Resolving Customer Conflicts with Respect and Authority

"Let's address the elephant in the room," began the CFO. "I've been reviewing the complaints about customer service. Apparently, some passengers feel we don't have enough staff to meet their needs. But honestly, with the prices we're charging, what more can they expect? They're lucky we're flying them from Point A to Point B."

Kelly, from Finance, chimed in. "Customers are always going to complain. But if we're saving money by cutting back on representatives, isn't that a win for us?"

Tim, who rarely spoke up, cleared his throat. "Actually, it's not. Every unresolved complaint damages our reputation. If we keep ignoring the issue, customers won't come back."

"So, what do you propose?" asked the CFO, skeptically.

Tim hesitated but said, "We need to focus on

de-escalation strategies and empowering staff to resolve conflicts quickly. Ignoring or mishandling complaints only makes things worse."

The CFO frowned but nodded reluctantly. "Fine. Let's hear some ideas."

## Why Conflict Management Matters

Conflict is inevitable in any customer service environment. However, how a business handles it can make the difference between losing a customer forever and turning a negative situation into a positive one. Poor conflict resolution leads to:

1. Loss of customer trust
2. Negative word-of-mouth or online reviews
3. Reduced employee morale
4. Potential public confrontations or viral incidents

Let's explore real-life examples of poor conflict resolution, followed by alternative approaches that prioritize respect, authority, and effective communication.

## Real-Life Examples: What NOT to Do

1. The Overbooking Incident: A major airline faced public backlash when a passenger was forcibly removed from a flight due to overbooking. The situation escalated because the airline refused

to offer reasonable alternatives and resorted to physical removal instead of negotiating.

**Better Alternative:**

- *Transparency*: Inform passengers at the gate about overbooking and offer incentives (e.g., travel vouchers, accommodations) to voluntarily give up their seat.
- *Empathy*: Apologize sincerely and communicate clearly about the situation.
- *Authority with Respect*: Train staff to remain calm and professional, even if passengers express frustration. What makes customers more frustrated is representative incompetence, lack of care or speaking in jargon or insincere company provided talking points.

2. **The Broken Promise**: A customer booked a rental car online, only to find the vehicle unavailable upon arrival. When they complained, the representative simply shrugged uncaringly and said, "There's nothing I can do."

**Better Alternative:**

- **Immediate Solutions**: Offer a level-up vehicle or partner with another agency to find one.
- **Compensation**: Provide discounts, upgrades, or future credits to show goodwill.

- **Ownership**: Empower employees to resolve the issue on the spot instead of deflecting responsibility.

3. The Rude Return Policy: A shopper tried to return a defective product but was met with a dismissive employee who cited store policy without showing understanding or flexibility.

**Better Alternative**:

- **Policy + Empathy**: While policies are important, they should be communicated with compassion. For example: "I understand this is frustrating. Let me see how I can help within our guidelines."
- **Win-Win Solutions**: Offer store credit or a replacement item as a gesture of goodwill.

Strategies for Handling Customer Conflicts

1. **Start with Empathy and Active Listening**
Customers want to feel heard. Even if their frustration is misplaced, acknowledging their feelings can diffuse tension. For example:
    - Wrong Approach: "That's not my problem."
    - Right Approach: "I'm really sorry you're experiencing this. Let's see what we can do to resolve it."

2. **Empower Employees with Authority**

Staff should have the autonomy to resolve common issues without escalating to a manager. This includes:
- Offering small compensations (e.g., discounts or vouchers)
- Approving reasonable returns or exchanges
- Providing direct resolutions the first time instead of transferring customers multiple times

3. **De-Escalation Techniques**: Train employees to manage upset customers calmly and assertively:
- Stay Calm: Keep a neutral tone, even if the customer raises their voice.
- Set Boundaries: If a customer becomes abusive, politely but firmly state: "I'm here to help, but I need us to keep this conversation respectful."
- Focus on Solutions: Redirect the conversation toward resolving the issue rather than dwelling on the problem.

4. Provide Clear Communication: Ambiguity frustrates customers. Be upfront about what can and cannot be done, and offer realistic timelines for solutions. For example:
- "Your refund has been processed and should appear in your account within 3-5 business days."

5. Follow Up After resolving a conflict, reach out to the customer to ensure satisfaction. This extra

step can turn a disgruntled customer into a loyal advocate.

## Encouraging Respect and Authority Without Escalation

A common misconception is that "The customer is always right." While customers deserve respect, businesses must also uphold reasonable policies and protect employees from unreasonable demands. Here's how to balance the two:

- **Set Expectations**: Clearly outline policies during the purchase or booking process.
- **Train for Assertiveness**: Equip employees with strategies to handle pushback while maintaining professionalism.
- **Offer Escalation Paths**: Provide clear steps for customers to escalate their concerns to higher management if necessary.

## Building a Culture of Conflict Resolution

Handling conflicts effectively starts with creating a company culture that values:

- **Proactive Problem-Solving:** Anticipate potential issues and address them before they escalate.
- **Continuous Training:** Invest in regular training programs on customer service, communication, and de-escalation.

- **Employee Well-Being**: Support staff with adequate resources, manageable workloads, and recognition for their efforts.
- **Customer-Centric Policies**: Design policies that prioritize fairness and transparency.

## The Ripple Effect of Better Conflict Management

When conflicts are handled well, the benefits extend beyond the individual customer:

- Higher Customer Retention: Satisfied customers are more likely to return and recommend your business.
- Positive Reputation: Effective conflict resolution can lead to glowing reviews and a stronger brand image.
- Improved Employee Morale: Empowered employees feel more confident and motivated, reducing turnover.

By addressing conflicts with empathy, authority, and a solutions-focused mindset, businesses can transform challenging situations into opportunities for growth. The next time a conflict arises, remember: how you handle it can say more about your company than the products or services you offer.

Reviews of the F------ airline are when things went wrong such as gate changes or flight delays, there were no representatives to assist. Even once a representative was found, customers tried to explain their concerns, but the agent rudely shut them down and treated them in such a condescending manner that they were humiliated. The agent's complete lack of manners and lack of professionalism made an already stressful experience even worse.

# CHAPTER 7
## Who's Piloting This Plane, Anyway?

Good morning, team.

Yesterday, HR blessed me with the gift of a very *enlightening* meeting. It seems that our turnover rate is causing some concern. Imagine that. HR thinks it's a problem when employees leave faster than passengers deplaning after a four-hour tarmac delay.

Now, I ask you, isn't working in the skies every kid's dream?
When I was young, we all wanted to fly on airplanes all day.

Yet, here we are, hemorrhaging employees. Why? Could someone please explain why they aren't grateful for the amazing opportunity we provide? Anyone?

...Silence.

"Alright, let me break it down for you. We're offering

these fine folks a *path into the skies*. Those other airlines would never hire these people. If it weren't for us, most of them would be flipping burgers or managing fryer oil at the local chain restaurant. This is a step *up*! Isn't it?"

Barely, sir.

"Excuse me?"

Uh... Yes, sir.

"Exactly. And these managers? Don't get me started. They have a template for discipline and still can't keep their staff in line! Discipline is key. Just like children need rules, so do employees. If they can't stick with us, we'll bring in younger, cheaper replacements. That's efficiency. Meeting adjourned."

*What just happened?*

You might call it a "leadership style." I'd call it... turbulence.

---

## Inspiring, Not Managing

Leadership isn't easy, and not everyone is built for it. That's okay. Leadership and management are as different as turbulence and smooth skies. Both exist, but only one leaves people feeling confident in the journey.

When I got my first management role at the age of 18, I was handed the honorary clipboard and told, "You're in charge." I had no idea what I was doing, but I sure *looked* the part. Clipboard in hand, I strutted around like a peacock, bossing around people who knew their jobs better than I did.

Did it earn me respect? Not a chance.

Real leadership isn't about appearances; it's about connection. It's about proving, day in and day out, that you're invested in the success and well-being of your team. It's about understanding this simple truth: **people work for people, not companies.**

---

### Leadership Lessons from the Skies

Let's revisit our airline CFO, shall we? His focus is on dollars, not people. He doesn't see employees as assets to be nurtured, but as numbers on a spreadsheet. His motto might as well be, *"Follow the rules and shut up."* Employees sense this lack of care, and guess what? They do the bare minimum until something better comes along.

Contrast that with a boss I once had. He was a leader in every sense of the word. He inspired me, challenged me, and valued my contributions. To this day, I'd drop everything to help him if he called.

That's the kind of loyalty real leadership creates.

But I've also experienced the opposite. I once worked under someone whose motto was "Good is good enough." That mindset drained the energy out of the entire organization. When I tried to go above and beyond, I was reprimanded for stepping outside the lines. Eventually, I knew it was time to move on.

If you're feeling undervalued, ask yourself:

- Am I seeing the situation clearly?
- Have I communicated my feelings to my manager or colleagues, but nothing changed?
- Have I done everything I can to improve this?

When the answer to all three is yes, and nothing has changed, it's time to chart a new course. But leave with dignity, and don't jump without a parachute (or, in this case, a new source of income lined up).

## The Top 3 Traits of Exceptional Leaders

Whether you're a seasoned captain or just earning your wings, here are three keys to exceptional leadership:

### 1. Humility

Great leaders ask their teams, *"How can I serve you better?"* Listen to their feedback. Grow from it. When employees feel heard and valued, they'll give you their best.

### 2. Clear Communication

We've all been there: You say something once and expect it to stick, only to be baffled when it doesn't. Here's the truth: Most people need to hear something **seven times** before it truly registers. So, communicate. Then communicate again.

**3. Trust and Empowerment**
No one likes to be micromanaged. Trust your team to do their jobs, and they'll rise to the occasion. If they stumble, be there to guide them—not to punish.

---

**Lessons from the Ground and Air**

The best leaders inspire loyalty, foster growth, and communicate with transparency. When employees feel valued, they stick around. When they feel disposable, they leave.

At that F------ Airline, they might have low fares, but they can't afford low morale. Leadership, like flying, requires preparation, skill, and a steady hand on the controls. Otherwise, it's not just the passengers who will look for another airline—it's the crew too.

---

**Are poor employees hired or created (nature or nurture)?**

One of the perennial questions in customer service is whether poor employees are born that way or if they are a product of their environment. It's a classic nature versus nurture debate, and the answer likely lies somewhere in the middle.

**Factors Contributing to Poor Employee Performance:**

- ***Weak Leadership***: A lack of strong, supportive leadership can significantly impact employee morale and performance. Without clear expectations, guidance, and recognition, employees may feel undervalued and unmotivated.

- ***Poor Training***: Inadequate training can leave employees ill-equipped to handle customer interactions effectively. If employees don't understand the company's values, products, or services, they are more likely to make mistakes and frustrate customers.

- ***Toxic Work Environment***: A negative work culture, characterized by high stress, lack of work-life balance, and poor communication, can lead to burnout and decreased productivity.

- ***Lack of Empowerment***: When employees aren't supporterd but feel micromanaged and unable to make decisions, they may become disengaged and resentful.

**How to Prevent Employees from Becoming Disengaged:**

- ***Hire the Right People***: While a positive work environment can significantly impact employee performance, it's crucial to start with a strong foundation. Hire individuals who align with the company's values and possess the skills necessary to excel in customer service roles. More than skills, hire for character. Skills can be taught.

- ***Invest in Training and Development***: Provide ongoing training to keep employees up-to-date on industry trends, product knowledge, and customer service best practices.

- ***Foster a Positive Work Culture***: Create a supportive and inclusive work environment where employees feel valued and appreciated.

- ***Empower Employees***: Give employees the authority to make decisions and solve problems.

- ***Recognize and Reward Performance***: Implement a flexible recognition program to reward employees for their hard work and dedication. Not all employees want public recognition or even a monetary reward. Some may want freedom to expand or opportunities to train others or grow in the company.

If you are new to an organization or have recently come to the realization that your team is not performing well, let's talk about turning the situation around.

**Turning Around Poor-Performing Employees:**

- *Identify the Root Cause*: Determine the underlying reasons for the employee's poor performance. Is it a lack of training, a personal issue, or a problem with the work environment?

- *Provide Coaching and Mentorship*: Offer guidance and support to help the employee improve their skills and performance. This could be an excellent opportunity for those employees who want the opportunity to expand their role.

- *Set Clear Expectations*: Clearly communicate performance expectations and provide regular feedback.

- *Offer Additional Training*: If necessary, provide additional training to help the employee develop the necessary skills.

- *Consider a Change in Role or Responsibilities*: If the employee is struggling in their current role, consider reassigning them to a different position that better suits their skills and interests.

- ***If All Else Fails, Consider Termination***: In some cases, it may be necessary to terminate an employee who consistently underperforms, or becomes toxic to other teammates, despite efforts to improve their performance.

By addressing the root causes of poor employee performance and implementing effective strategies to improve employee engagement and satisfaction, businesses can create a customer service culture that drives customer loyalty and business success.

**Reviews of the F------ airline are overwhelming complaints from past and current employees that policies are not clearly communicated, and paychecks are short without cause. The leadership of low morals was clear at the ground floor which amplifies the low morale. Employees feel that listing this company on their resume would cause more harm in trying to get a job with another airline (no one would want the lack of experience and low morale they gain at this company) and not help them get experience in the airline industry.**

# CHAPTER 8
## The Ripple Effect of Quiet Quitting

The meeting room was unusually quiet. It was as though the energy had been vacuumed out of the space.

Tim, one of the airline's operations managers, sat with his arms crossed, eyes fixed on his notebook. When the CFO called on him for input, he simply shrugged.

"Tim, do you have anything to add about how we can improve efficiency?"

He hesitated, then answered flatly, "Not really. What's the point? Any idea I have usually gets shot down, and even if it's implemented, it's not like anyone recognizes the effort."

The room shifted uncomfortably.

"Well," the CFO responded, clearly annoyed, "if you don't care, maybe it's time to reassess whether you belong here."

Tim sighed. "I do care. I used to care a lot. I have shared countless ideas that I know would work but they are either shut down or ignored. If the idea is not about automating or minimizing service, no one wants to listen. Not to mention, things like asking if I could leave an hour early to attend my son's game, the request was denied for no good reason. No one cares here, why should I? It's not worth it to stay motivated."

The CFO dismissed Tim's comment with a wave of his hand, but the exchange lingered in the air.

Unbeknownst to leadership, Tim's attitude wasn't an isolated case—it was an undercurrent running through the airline, a symptom of the quiet quitting culture taking root.

## The Quiet Quitting Culture: A Silent Threat to Business

Quiet quitting, or the act of doing the bare minimum to get by at work, isn't always about laziness. Often, it stems from a deeper disconnection between employees and their workplace.

At F----- Airlines, a company already riddled with operational inefficiencies and a reputation for poor customer service, this culture was the final nail in the coffin.

Tim's disengagement wasn't born out of a lack of ability—it was nurtured by a system that failed to inspire or value him. For employees like Tim, doing more felt futile because their contributions went unrecognized, and the leadership's focus was solely on squeezing out profits at any cost.

## The Bigger Picture: How Quiet Quitting Impacts Customers

When employees feel undervalued, their lack of engagement often trickles down to the customer experience. Often times employees are treated differently than customers. Always treat your employees the way you want them to treat your customers, but at F----- Airlines, this looked like:

1. **Delayed Responses:** Employees took their time addressing customer inquiries, leading to longer wait times and more frustrated passengers.

2. **Indifferent Service:** Flight attendants and ground staff became less proactive, doing only what was explicitly required—no more, no less. Passengers noticed the lack of warmth, and it reinforced their perception of the airline as indifferent to their needs.

3. **Higher Turnover:** Disengaged employees either quietly stayed in their roles or left for

better opportunities. High turnover rates made it harder to maintain consistency in service and team cohesion.

4. **Reputational Damage:** Word spread among customers about the indifferent attitude of staff. Reviews labeled the airline as "unfeeling" or "robotic," further driving away potential customers.

In 2021, a fast-food chain experienced a surge in online complaints about slow service and rude staff. Internal reviews revealed that employees were overworked, underpaid, and rarely recognized for their efforts. By implementing a recognition program and increasing wages, the chain saw a dramatic improvement in customer satisfaction scores within six months.

A retail giant faced similar issues with disengaged employees. They introduced a mentoring program that paired new hires with experienced staff, fostering a sense of community and shared purpose. As a result, employee turnover dropped by 25%, and customers reported a noticeable improvement in service quality.

---

### Turning the Tide: Five Steps to Reignite Employee Engagement

To counteract the effects of quiet quitting, companies must first understand the root causes of disengagement. Here are five ways F----- Airlines—and any organization—could foster a positive work environment:

1. **Celebrate Employee Contributions**
   Recognize and reward employees for their ideas and efforts, both big and small. A public "thank you" or acknowledgment during meetings can go a long way in making employees feel valued. Implement programs where team members can nominate their peers for recognition.

A tech company introduced a "Shoutout Wall," where employees could publicly acknowledge their colleagues' achievements. This small gesture significantly boosted morale and teamwork. There are also companies where recognition can accumulate points that can be traded for gift cards.

2. **Offer Professional Development Opportunities**
   Invest in employees' growth through training, mentorship programs, and career development workshops. Show them that the company is committed to their long-term success, not just their immediate output.

A manufacturing firm partnered with local universities to offer free skill-building courses to employees. The initiative not only improved retention rates but also increased innovation as employees applied their new skills to workplace challenges.

### 3. Create a Feedback Loop

Regularly seek and act on employee feedback. Create forums where employees can voice their concerns and propose solutions without fear of retribution. More importantly, follow through on their suggestions when feasible to build trust.

A healthcare provider set up monthly "listening sessions" with frontline workers. By addressing common pain points raised in these sessions, the organization improved both employee satisfaction and patient outcomes.

### 4. Foster Cross-Functional Collaboration

Encourage departments to work together on projects that impact the entire company. For instance, flight attendants could partner with marketing teams to design more customer-friendly service protocols, creating a sense of shared purpose and ownership.

A global airline launched an initiative where employees from different departments shadowed each other for a day. This program increased empathy and understanding among teams, leading to smoother operations and a better customer experience.

5. **Build a Culture of Transparency and Trust**
   Be honest about the company's challenges and involve employees in solving them. Transparency about decision-making processes fosters trust and helps employees feel like valued contributors, not just cogs in a machine.

A financial services firm openly shared its struggles with employees during a market downturn. By involving staff in brainstorming solutions, they not only weathered the crisis but emerged stronger, with a more united workforce.

## The Power of Effective Teamwork and Communication

At its core, quiet quitting is a breakdown of trust and connection. To repair this, companies must prioritize teamwork and communication. When employees feel that their ideas are valued and their contributions matter, they're more likely to go above and beyond.

Imagine if Tim's concerns in that meeting had been met with genuine interest rather than dismissal. A simple response like, "Tim, I hear you. Let's discuss your ideas after this meeting," could have reignited his sense of purpose and motivated him to contribute.

When teams feel aligned and supported, they create a ripple effect that extends to the customer experience. Customers feel the difference when employees are energized and genuinely care about their needs.

### A Lesson for All Businesses

Quiet quitting doesn't happen in a vacuum—it's a direct reflection of a company's culture. For F----- Airlines, the cost of ignoring employee morale wasn't just disengaged staff; it was unhappy customers, lower revenue, and an eventual path toward irrelevance.

The lesson is clear: businesses that prioritize their employees will see the benefits reflected in every aspect of their operations. Employees who feel valued will, in turn, create exceptional experiences for customers and take the initiative to bring in new customers. And when customers are happy, success becomes inevitable.

**A recent review of the F------ airline was: The flight attendants seemed unmotivated and disengaged. "When I asked for help storing my bag, I was met**

with a shrug and told to "figure it out." The in-flight announcements were rushed and garbled.

# CHAPTER 9
## Why is Good Customer Service So Hard?

Good morning, everyone. Please take your seats—I'd like to start promptly today.

First, I owe you all an apology for my tone during last month's meeting. It's no excuse, but frustration got the best of me. I kept thinking about all we do for our employees—providing them jobs, training, and opportunities—and I couldn't understand why they didn't seem more appreciative.

That said, I did want to announce that Tim has decided to take a position at another company. We are thankful for his service at F------ Airlines.

Today we're shifting focus to something even more vital: **customer service**.

Let me be clear: if we're going to hit our numbers and get that Christmas bonus, we need to find ways to enhance customer service that don't cost us more money. Time is money, folks. If our employees are spending too much time with customers, they're costing us. So, let's find the middle ground. I want to hear ideas.

Kelly in Finance kicks things off.

"A service we already offer is helping our customers manage their finances. Why not expand on that? Our credit card program is fine, but we're missing opportunities. Think about it: an average of 200 potential cardholders on every flight, all sitting captive. The flight attendants aren't doing much at the end of the flight anyway—why not have them pitch the credit card? I can even draft a script!"

Mark from Operations jumps in next, grinning. "I get where Kelly's coming from, but I think self-service is the way forward. The less we're involved, the better. Let's expand self-check-in kiosks and let customers tag their own bags. If they run into issues, they can watch a video or use AI-powered chat support. It's efficient and... cost-effective!"

The CFO nods, clearly impressed. "Now we're thinking! If it weren't for those pesky FAA regulations, I'd suggest recording the safety instructions and swapping out flight attendants for vending machines to handle snacks. But hey, baby steps, right? Sometimes, good customer service just means staying out of the way."

---

Sound familiar?

If you've ever been on the receiving end of ideas like these, you know why good customer service feels harder to come by these days.

## What Happened to Customer Service?

The first draft of this book was written pre-pandemic, back when "Karen" was just a woman's name, and viral videos of customer meltdowns were still a novelty. Since then, everything has changed—work, attitudes, expectations.

We've entered an era of *quiet quitting*, *short tempers*, and *heightened frustrations*. Many people work remotely, avoiding commutes and cubicles, but also losing the small, daily interactions that build patience and empathy.

It's easy to blame the "Karens" in those viral clips, but have you ever stopped to wonder what led to their outbursts? Often, we only see the moment of meltdown, not the slow burn that preceded it.

Let me share two personal experiences that made me think: **How could this have been handled better?**

---

## The Drive-Thru Fiasco

The big appeal of a drive-thru is speed—you're hungry, you want food, *now*. One evening, I sent my adult son to grab dinner for us. He returned with our order, but my favorite item was missing. You know, the one I'd been looking forward to all day.

No big deal, right? Except I was *starving*.

Sure, my son could have checked the bag at the window, but he's a former fast-food employee and knew they track drive-thru times. Rushing off seemed considerate. Looking at the receipt, I saw we'd been charged for the missing item.

Annoying, but solvable.

I called the restaurant, calmly explained the situation, expecting a quick fix by requesting that they refund the missing item. It was only around $5 so I thought it would not be a big deal.

"Um, I don't think I can do that," said the employee. After some fumbling, unbeknownst to me, the manager got on the line.

"Hello" she blurted.

"Hello" I calmly replied.

"Yes…" was her response.

"I'm confused, who am I speaking with?" I asked.

"This is the manager."

Pause

"Oh, what you meant to say was, 'Hello, this is Tina, the manager. How can I help you?'" I might have been slightly snarky.

"Yes, what is the problem", she replied.

I took a breath, knowing my correction had no effect on her. After repeating my story, I asked again for a refund.

"We can't refund you," she said. "You can come back, and I will give you the item".

*Return to the restaurant?*

Many people drive through because they are going from one destination to another. They are not going back.

There was no in-store solution offered. No apology. No "if would you give me your address, I will be happy to mail you a gift card for the trouble". No solution whatsoever.

It wasn't until I called the district office that the issue was resolved—two coupons for free combo meals, a $30 value. But by then, my meal was cold, my evening was disrupted, I was still hungry, and the company lost 6 times what the missing item was worth, and they lost a customer. I no longer frequent that restaurant. All over a $5 item.

---

**Lessons Learned**

How could this have been handled better?

1. **More than a sincere apology, acknowledge the error.** Something as simple as, "I'm so sorry—we messed up," can go a long way in calming an upset customer.

2. **Empower employees.** If the corporation empowered the first employee to complete the refund (up to a limited amount, of course) or had the authority to offer a coupon or small credit, the issue could've been resolved in minutes. Rigid policies create bottlenecks. Empowering front-line employees to resolve common complaints without managerial approval can speed up resolutions and improve customer satisfaction.

3. **Understand your customers.** Drive-thru customers are in a hurry. A simple, immediate solution—like offering a digital gift card—would've turned this negative into a positive.

---

### The Five Below Disappointment

I fell in love with a game I played at a friend's house. It was sold exclusively at Five Below. Every time I passed a Five Below, I ran in to see if it was available. I finally decided to look online and was excited to find it available for in-store pickup nearby. Hours after my order should have been ready, I arrived to find the item wasn't there. Worse, no one had bothered to notify me.

I contacted customer service, spending hours via email (because of course there was no number to call) with back-and-forth explanation and negotiation only to be FINALLY offered a $5 gift card. By then, I was done!

My enthusiasm for the brand had evaporated. For $5, they not only lost me as a customer, but I wrote a book on customer service and used them by name as an example of what poor customer service is like.

What could they have done differently?

- **Communicate proactively.** A quick email or text notifying me the item was unavailable would've saved me a trip and frustration.

- **Offer a solution immediately.** Instead of making me negotiate for compensation, they could've offered the $5 gift card upfront. It would have saved me, the customer, time and aggravation and saved money on the customer service representative who spent way too much time dealing with the issue.

---

## Avoiding Viral Customer Service Nightmares

No one wants their company featured in the next viral "Karen" video, but avoiding that fate takes more than luck—it requires a proactive strategy for managing complaints effectively. Here's how to handle customer complaints with professionalism, empathy, and results.

**The Art of Handling Complaints**

**1. Start with empathy.**

When a customer is upset, they're not just reacting to the immediate issue—they may be dealing with a string of frustrations in their day, week, or even life. A simple acknowledgment of their feelings can defuse tension.

- **Example**: Imagine a passenger on F------- Airline whose flight has been delayed for hours. Instead of a generic apology, or using the words "sorry" or "I apologize", try:
  *"I understand how frustrating this delay must be, especially since I am sure you had plans or connections you're missing. We are going to do everything we can to make this right."*

This approach humanizes the interaction and shifts the focus to resolution.

**2. Empower and train your team.** Employees should have the tools and authority to solve problems quickly and effectively.

- **Anticipate issues.** Think ahead about

common complaints and have ready-made solutions, such as the fast-food example. Thankfully, humans are the ones who put the orders together. A missing item is going to happen sometimes. Have a plan path that everyone knows on how to solve that problem. For example, the first remedy is to see if the customer can come back. If yes, not only apologize but thank them for taking the time to return and offer a free drink or dessert for their trouble. If no, what is your next, fastest solution?

- **Act with empathy.** Customers aren't just numbers—they're people. Treat them with understanding, and you'll build loyalty instead of resentment.

Remember, the goal isn't just to resolve issues but to leave customers feeling valued. In a world where frustrations run high, small acts of care and competence can set your business apart.

### 3. Be transparent about next steps.

Uncertainty fuels frustration. Customers want to know *what will happen next* and *how long it will take*.

- **Example**: At a restaurant with a missing order item, instead of saying, "I can't do that," it would be better to say, *"I am going to escalate this to my manager right now. I don't have the authorization to do refunds. Would*

> *you give me 5 minutes to take care of this for you?"*

Being honest about limitations while clearly communicating a path forward builds trust. Customers remember how quickly and effectively their concerns were resolved, not just the original problem.

### 4. Close the loop.

No one likes admitting mistakes or facing conflict, but every complaint deserves follow-up to ensure the customer feels heard and valued. After the initial resolution, reach out to confirm satisfaction.

> - **Example**: A day after issuing a refund for a missed food order, a manager should contact the customer to say:
>   *"Hi, this is Tina from The Restaurant. I wanted to make sure you received your refund and were satisfied with how we resolved the issue. Thank you for giving us another chance."*

Customers will remember the remedy more than they will remember the initial issue.

### 5. Measure Customer Satisfaction (CSAT):

Measuring customer satisfaction is key and everyone at your company should be on board and aware of where you stand and what steps you are taking to improve your scores. There should be an internal system in place for customers to rate their satisfaction, especially after resolving a complaint. This metric directly measures how happy customers are with the resolution.

- **Example Question**: "Missteps in your service with us is never our intention but on a scale of 1 to 5, how satisfied were you with how we handled your issue today?"
- **Goal**: Maintain an average CSAT score of 4.5 or higher.

**Net Promoter Score (NPS):**

NPS measures how likely customers are to recommend your business to others. A high NPS indicates strong customer loyalty, even after a complaint.

- **Example Question**: "On a scale of 0 to 10, how likely are you to recommend us to a friend or colleague based on how we resolved your issue?"
- **Tip**: Follow up with detractors (those who rate you 0–6) to understand what went wrong and how to improve.

**Complaint Volume and Trends:**

Track the number of complaints over time and

identify patterns.

- **Example**: Are you receiving repeated complaints about delayed flights or missing food items?
- **Action**: Use this data to address systemic issues. For example, if a restaurant consistently forgets items in orders, review packaging processes and train staff to double-check.

---

**Average Resolution Time:**

How long does it take to resolve complaints? Faster resolutions lead to happier customers and more efficient operations.

- **Goal**: Depending on the product or service you provide, the goal to resolve most complaints should be to resolve it after the first communication about the mistake. This could be on the first call or email that made you aware of the issue.

---

**Customer Retention Post-Complaint:**

Measure how many customers return after filing a complaint. This shows whether your resolution efforts are effective in rebuilding trust.

- **Tip**: Offer incentives, like discounts or loyalty points, to encourage repeat business after resolving an issue.

Handling complaints isn't just damage control —it's an opportunity to create loyal customers who sing your praises. By focusing on empathy, empowerment, and measurable results, you can transform your customer service from reactive to proactive, leaving even your most frustrated customers saying, "Wow, they really care."

**Reviews of the F------ airline are overwhelming statements such as, "The credit card sales pitch at the end of the flight felt more enthusiastic than any actual service provided.**
**I would happily pay more to be treated kindly, not lose my bags, know I have a decent seat, have the confidence that there will be staff there to help me when I need it and not have the stress they caused me".**

# CHAPTER 10
## The Role of Technology in Customer Service

The F------- Airline boardroom was abuzz with the next big idea. Facing mounting pressure to cut costs and boost profits, the leadership turned their attention to technology.

"Ladies and gentlemen," the CFO began, "we have a clear path forward: automation. Chatbots, self-service kiosks, AI-powered FAQs—these tools can significantly reduce our payroll expenses and improve efficiency.

Who needs human agents when customers can solve their own problems?"

The room nodded in collective agreement, eager to embrace a tech-heavy approach.

Kelly, always enthusiastic, chimed in. "Think about it! We could cut frontline staff by half and replace them with virtual assistants. Customers can book, cancel, and rebook their flights without ever speaking to a human. And if they have questions, a chatbot can handle them."

Junior added, "We could also add QR codes everywhere—on the seat backs, at check-in counters, even on our snacks. Everything the customer needs is at their fingertips. If they're confused, they can scan the code and find a how-to video. No need for our staff to get involved."

The CFO concluded, "This is about efficiency and cost savings. More automation means fewer errors and less dependency on unreliable employees. Let's empower customers to serve themselves."

While the plan looked promising on paper, its execution was a different story.

### The Fallout of Over-Automation

A year into the full automation rollout, F------- Airline's customer satisfaction scores plummeted to historic lows.

Passengers were frustrated by unresponsive chatbots that couldn't understand nuanced issues. Self-service kiosks malfunctioned frequently, leaving long lines of angry travelers. And the QR codes? They worked… sometimes under the right lighting conditions.

One viral incident showcased the chaos: A family of four missed their connecting flight due to a mechanical delay. They sought help at a self-service kiosk, which directed them to a chatbot on the app. The chatbot, unable to grasp the urgency, suggested booking a hotel for the night—but provided no way to do so. By the time the family found a human employee (after hours of searching), the next available flight was three days later. The story, captured in a tearful video, garnered millions of views and cemented F------- Airline's reputation as a faceless corporation that prioritized cost-cutting over customer care.

Meanwhile, loyalty eroded. Customers turned to competitors who still offered live support. Even employees felt the sting, as their roles became increasingly limited to troubleshooting technology rather than helping people. Morale dropped, and turnover skyrocketed.

### The Benefits of Technology—When Done Right

Technology isn't inherently the villain. In fact, when used thoughtfully, it can enhance customer service:

1. ***Efficiency for Simple Tasks***: Chatbots and self-service portals excel at handling straightforward requests, such as checking flight status, reprinting boarding passes, or updating personal information.

2. ***24/7 Availability***: Automated systems can provide round-the-clock assistance,

ensuring customers can access help anytime, anywhere.

3. ***Data Insights***: AI tools can analyze customer interactions to identify pain points, enabling businesses to proactively address common issues.

However, the key to success lies in balance. Technology should augment human service—not replace it entirely.

---

### *Revolutionizing Service: A Human-Centered Approach*

To rebuild trust and loyalty, businesses must prioritize human connection. Here's how:

#### 1. *Personalized Service*

Automation can't replicate the warmth of human interaction. Customers want to feel heard and valued, especially during complex or emotional situations. Personalized service builds trust and fosters long-term loyalty.

For example, imagine a passenger calling F------- Airline about a lost piece of luggage. Instead of navigating an endless phone tree, they're connected to a trained agent who listens empathetically, tracks the bag, and follows up until it's returned. That's the kind of service people remember.

While they are still used everywhere, to

revolutionize customer service, the days of "Press 1 for this. Press 2 for that" will have to go away and become as irrelevant as the rotary phone. If you are not familiar with this lovely rotary phone (my favorite was in the avocado green color), I highly recommend doing your own research on this antiquated gem of a device.

## 2. *Effective Training Programs*

Great customer service starts with well-trained employees. Training should go beyond basic procedures to include:

- *Conflict Resolution*: Equip staff to handle difficult situations calmly and effectively.
- *Empathy Exercises*: Teach employees to see issues from the customer's perspective.
- *Continuous Learning*: Regular workshops and refresher courses ensure skills stay sharp.

## 3. *Coaching and Mentoring*

Pairing new hires with experienced mentors fosters a culture of excellence. Ongoing coaching helps employees refine their skills, stay motivated and be encouraged in their work.

## 4. *Minimizing Turnover*

High turnover disrupts service consistency. To retain top talent, businesses should:

- Offer competitive wages and benefits.
- Create opportunities for growth and advancement.
- Recognize and reward outstanding performance.

### 5. *Blending Technology with Humanity*

Instead of replacing employees, use technology to support them. For instance:

- *AI-Assisted Tools*: Provide agents with real-time data and suggested solutions during calls, enabling faster and more accurate responses.

- *Self-Service with a Safety Net*: If you are not ready to leap into a full human experience, allow customers to start with a self-service option but offer an easy transition to a live agent if needed.

## Building a Culture of Care

The lesson from F------- Airline's missteps is clear: Cost-cutting at the expense of human connection is a losing strategy.

Businesses thrive when they prioritize people—both customers and employees.

By leveraging technology thoughtfully, investing in training and development, and fostering a culture of care, companies can revolutionize customer service. It's not just about solving problems; it's about creating positive, memorable experiences that build loyalty and trust.

In the end, customer service is about more than profits. It's about treating people with dignity and respect, creating connections, and making the world a little kinder—one interaction at a time.

**Reviews of the F------ airline are that their technology is antiquated. There is no way to track your bags like other airlines offer. The information on the website and at the airport regarding gate and baggage information is often incorrect.**

# CHAPTER 11
## Lessons from the Brink

It didn't have to end this way for F-------Airline. Yet, the final meeting before the company's bankruptcy filing was eerily similar to those that had come before—an obsession with cutting costs, increasing revenue through gimmicks, and sidestepping genuine customer engagement.

As the CFO delivered the dismal quarterly report, the room was tense. "We missed our targets again," he said. "Passenger volume is down, and our customer satisfaction scores are at an all-time low. Our credit card partnership is failing to bring in the revenue we projected. And most importantly, we're dangerously close to defaulting on our debts."

Kelly from finance, once so enthusiastic about pitching credit cards to a captive audience, sighed. "We can't even get flight attendants to follow the script anymore. They're too overwhelmed by customer complaints. No one wants to be trapped on a plane being forced to listen to a long commercial with flight attendants pushing applications in their face."

Mark, who had championed self-service kiosks, added, "We thought automation would save money, but it backfired.

Customers are frustrated when the kiosks break or don't solve their issues. They're flooding our call centers, which are understaffed and overwhelmed."

The CFO leaned back in his chair, his face a mixture of frustration and resignation. "We did everything we could to save money and boost revenue. Why isn't it working?"

No one had the courage to say it outright, but the truth was obvious: the company had forgotten the very people who kept it in business—its customers and employees.

By prioritizing short-term gains over long-term loyalty, F-------Airline had alienated both groups, creating a cycle of dissatisfaction and decline.

---

**Lessons Learned**

The story of F-------Airline serves as a cautionary tale, but it's also a call to action. Businesses don't have to follow the same path. Here are the key lessons to take away:

1. *Customer Experience Is Everything*

F-------Airline's downfall began when it devalued the customer experience. Customers don't just buy products or services; they invest in experiences. Whether it's a smooth flight, a friendly interaction, or a quick resolution to a problem, every touchpoint matters.

- Takeaway: Prioritize the customer journey from start to finish. Invest in training employees to deliver excellent service, empower them to resolve issues on the spot, and listen to feedback to continually improve.

## 2. *Empathy Is Not a Cost*

One of the most glaring failures at F-------Airline was its lack of empathy. The company viewed customer complaints as nuisances rather than opportunities to build trust and loyalty.

- Takeaway: Treat every customer interaction as a chance to show you care. A sincere gesture of goodwill can turn a dissatisfied customer into a lifelong advocate.

## 3. *Short-Term Thinking Leads to Long-Term Pain*

The airline's relentless focus on cutting costs and boosting short-term profits came at the expense of long-term sustainability. By neglecting customer and employee satisfaction, it created a toxic culture that eventually led to its demise.

> - Takeaway: Balance immediate financial goals with investments in people and processes that ensure long-term success. Happy employees lead to happy customers, which leads to business growth.

### 4. *Innovation Must Serve the Customer*

Automation and self-service tools can enhance efficiency, but only if they meet customer needs. F-------Airline's kiosks and AI chatbots frustrated more customers than they helped because they were implemented as cost-cutting measures rather than service enhancements.

> - Takeaway: Use technology to enhance, not replace, the human element. Always test new tools from the customer's perspective and ensure there's a backup plan when technology fails.

### 5. *Employees Are Your Frontline Advocates*

Disengaged employees can't deliver great service. F-------Airline's staff were overworked, undertrained, and unsupported, leading to high turnover and poor morale.

> - Takeaway: Invest in your employees. Provide them with the training, tools, and autonomy they need to excel. Recognize and reward their contributions and create a

culture where they feel valued.

## Moving Forward: A Culture of Service

The downfall of F-------Airline is not just a story about poor customer service; it's a reminder of the broader impact businesses can have on society. When companies prioritize profit over people, they don't just lose customers—they miss an opportunity to serve a need in the community and make the world a better place.

An airline that offered a low-cost option is needed in the marketplace for families or emergencies such as a death of a loved one.

What if, instead of doubling down on cost-cutting, F-------Airline had chosen a different path? Imagine a company where they understood their purpose was to serve the people who are underserved?

What if every employee is trained to see themselves as an ambassador of kindness and professionalism. Where complaints are viewed not as problems but as opportunities to shine. Where the goal isn't just to make a sale but to make a connection.

This isn't a pipe dream. Many businesses have embraced a culture of service and reaped the rewards, not just in profits but in reputation, employee satisfaction, and customer loyalty.

### *Here's how you can, too:*

1. ***Lead with Purpose***

Start with a mission that goes beyond making money. Ask yourself: What impact do you want your business to have on the world? Use this purpose to guide every decision, from hiring practices to customer interactions.

2. ***Foster a Culture of Caring***

Create an environment where employees feel empowered to go the extra mile for customers. Celebrate acts of kindness and innovation, and encourage employees to bring their whole selves to work.

3. ***Be the Change***

As a leader, model the behavior you want to see. Treat your employees and customers with respect and empathy, and hold yourself accountable for upholding your company's values.

4. ***Measure What Matters***

You cannot improve what you cannot measure. Track metrics that reflect your commitment to service, such as customer satisfaction, employee engagement, and repeat business. Use these insights to continuously improve.

5. ***Embrace Community***

Businesses don't operate in isolation. They're part of a larger ecosystem of customers, employees, suppliers, and neighbors. By prioritizing relationships over transactions, you can build a network of goodwill that supports your business through good times and bad.

## A Vision for the Future

The world is hungry for connection, compassion, and community. By revolutionizing how we serve each other, businesses have the power to meet this need and create a ripple effect of positive change. Good customer service isn't just about increasing profits; it's about making the world a better place, one interaction at a time.

As you finish this book, I encourage you to take what you've learned and put it into practice. Whether you're a business owner, manager, or employee, you have the power to make a difference.

Start small: greet each customer with a smile, listen more than you speak, and look for opportunities to go above and beyond by serving something and someone greater than yourself.

Let's be the change we want to see. Let's build businesses and communities that prioritize people over profits. Let's create a culture of service that transforms not just companies but lives. Together, we can prove that kindness is not a weakness—it's the greatest strength of all.

**It took a while to find any positive reviews on F------- Airlines. The most positive review was that the price was good except everything that came with that price made the price not worth it.**

If you need help refocusing your business, reach out to one of our coaches at www.theriteservice.com

www.ingramcontent.com/pod-product-compliance
Lightning Source LLC
Chambersburg PA
CBHW070342230526
45471CB00006B/2418